TABLE OF CC

TABLE OF CONTENTS 1

Dedication 9

CHAPTER 1: SELF-LOVE, HEALING
AND HAPPINESS 1

CHAPTER 2: SINGLE AND SELF-
LOVE 8

CHAPTER 3: LOVE YOURSELF
FROM THE INSIDE OUT 13

CHAPTER 4: TRUE BEAUTY LIES
WITHIN 21

CHAPTER 5: KNOW YOUR WORTH ..
32

CHAPTER 6: HAVE AN ATTITUDE
OF GRATITUDE 39

CHAPTER 7: BE BOLD, BE CONFI-
DENT 45

CHAPTER 8: HAPPINESS IS FOUND
IN THE MOMENTS 52

CHAPTER 9: DARE TO DREAM BIG
AND NEVER QUIT! 57

CHAPTER 10: BE FABULOUS! 61

CHAPTER 11: LET CONFUSION BE
A THING OF THE PAST! 67

AUTHOR BIO 74

NOTE FROM THE AUTHOR 76

THE SECRET RULES OF SELF-LOVE: HOW TO LOVE YOURSELF, OVERCOME THE LONELINESS OF BEING SINGLE, AND ACHIEVE HAPPINESS

BY WINSOME CAMPBELL-GREEN

THE SECRET RULES OF SELF-LOVE:
HOW TO LOVE YOURSELF, OVERCOME
THE LONELINESS OF BEING SINGLE,
AND ACHIEVE HAPPINESS

OTHER BOOKS WRITTEN BY WINSOME
CAMPBELL-GREEN

- HIGH HEELS IN TECH: WOMEN,
  TECHNOLOGY AND CHANGE

- TEN LIFE CHANGING LESSONS

- THE PERKS OF A POSITIVE ATTI-
  TUDE: A PRACTICAL GUIDE TO
  HAPPINESS AND SUCCESS

- FABULOSITY IS YOU: A WOMAN'S
  GUIDE FOR FASHION TIPS,
  WEIGHT-LOSS TIPS, SKIN CARE
  SECRETS, RELATIONSHIPS AND
  PURSUING HER PURPOSE

VISIT THE WEBSITE: WWW.CGWRIT-
INGSERVICES.COM

Dear Readers,

We each have our own experiences in life, which shapes our perspectives. However, your own experiences, and that of others, offer insight and clarity into some of the situation you are facing. I was inspired to write this book to help men and women who are living a life defined by loneliness, rejection, disappointment and lack of purpose to find healing and happiness. The truth is many people are hurting and they do not know they need healing. Unless you come to the realisation, healing hurts and wounds is a process. To be re-born into self-love will be a process. The rules and lessons I shared in this book is steps I have used in my own life. In this book, I show you why it's so important to love and accept yourself without judgment or conceit. Your happiness, joy, peace and healing begin when you can confront self-pity. There is no need to criticise yourself. I have included some practical tips to help boost your self-esteem and your self-approval. You can read this book in one go or you can savour the journey and read each chapter daily. How often can you read this book? It's perfectly okay to read and re-read this book and suggest it to your friends, sisters, mothers, aunts and others.

-Author, Winsome Campbell-Green

Dedication

Dedicated to the women who raised me:

MY LOVING SISTERS,

*who've been a rock of stability throughout
my entire life…*

MY AMAZING MOTHER,

the woman who gave life to me, whose loving spirit, powerful prayers and unwavering support sustains me still…

CHAPTER 1: SELF-LOVE, HEALING AND HAPPINESS

Self-love is the underpinning of happiness. It requires you to eliminate stress and low self-esteem. To be self-approved you must let go of what does not serve your purpose. Adopt an attitude of confidence without being conceited. To love others, you must love yourself first. Overcome any obstacle in your way and face any challenge with boldness. Know your worth, value yourself and always expect excellence in your life and in your interaction with family and friends.

Have you ever felt you are not living up to your true potential? It could be you are lacking self-love. Being conceited or showering yourself with self-praise is not self-love. Self-love can only operate in your life when you become self-approved. Self-approval is to approve your own actions and character based on your judgment. It means any distractions or any obstacles will not intimidate you. By holding unto thoughts and situations that cause stress, you leave no room for loving yourself. Learn to build your self-esteem and raise your standards. How you think about yourself and allow others to treat you will determine if you have a high self-esteem. Without self-esteem, self-love is not possible. To have self-love is to let go of what does not serve your true purpose. There is power in releasing any baggage that blocks opportunities for personal advancement or love in your life. Love yourself first to love others.

A few years ago I experienced lack of self-love. I thought I knew what loving myself meant until I was working and living on my own. I felt I needed people around me to feel complete. However, my most telling moments were when I had time to myself to think and reflect. I felt gripped by loneliness even though I friends and family were only a phone call away. I was still perplexed by the fact that I had to work before entering university. I ignored my accomplishments and questioned every setback. Instead of using my time outside work to explore my passions, hobbies, and purpose, I was busy living in the past. I needed a sharp reminder to do something good with my time. However, it was a huge obstacle for me to overcome. One day I decided to do something wonderful for myself. I used my free time to explore nature by going to the beach, reading motivational books, modelling, exercising to keep fit and other activities that required me to have the courage and determination. This led to me discover new passions and built my confidence. Discovering that there is no limit to what I can do, gave me greater courage. I did everything with confidence. By getting to know myself I could embrace me. It's possible to celebrate your accomplishments without having a false sense of pride. The truth is I needed to see myself as others did: a strong, confident, happy and kind young woman. Once I began to embrace these qualities about myself, I started to feel comfortable and happy within. As a result of these significant experiences, I am able to encourage love and abundant blessings in my life, and in family and friends. Therefore, self-love for me is really an appreciation of what was, what is and knowing what will come is just a bonus.

You cannot just exist in a life without love and self-respect. There is no reason to be ashamed that you may lack self-love. Some people experience lack of self-love at one point in his or her life. It's no surprise that many educated women and men lack self-love. The rise of teenage pregnancy, pedophiles, rape, incest, molestation, and suicide are all telling indications that there is no love of self. Oftentimes, these acts demonstrate a need to feel in control. You need to realise that it takes a strong person to bare all vulnerabilities, accept his or her flaws and work on healing his or her life. Too many young men resort to crime, drugs and casual relationships where they hurt young women and themselves. Similarly, some young women declare defeat over their lives and decide they are not worthy. Just remember these words: "You are enough for you."

CHAPTER 2: SINGLE AND SELF-LOVE

Take comfort in being single because greater things are ahead. To rush into long-term relationships without self-love can be disastrous. Some women find themselves in abusive relationships (physical and emotional). If you look on the patterns of events in your life, you will realise it's not a "coincidence". Go back into the far reaches of your mind and you may find many past events where you will find some hurt that resulted in low self-esteem. The foundation for this was already laid from earlier in your life. You moved blindly through your life with the same lacking mindset. Therefore, you attract a partner with similar qualities. One of the root causes of domestic violence is because the partner wants to be in control and overcompensate by inflicting harm. I do realise this is a very sensitive issue for many women across the world and it must be examined on an individual basis. However, I am concerned when others say some women "subjected" themselves to domestic abuse. I say, be mindful of whom you become involved with. Get to know each other before making any commitment. Take time to understand each other's core values. On the other hand, I believe that if you are hurting someone emotionally or physically, examine the reasons behind your emotions. Jealousy is a symptom of lack of self-love. Once you know that you have resolved any past hurts, there is no need to harm others. As a woman, break any habit of speaking self-deflating comments about yourself. I believe if you feel comfortable associating derogatory comments to yourself, then your self-esteem needs to be fixed. Never degrade yourself.

Too many men suffer from lack of self-love. This issue is most prevalent with middle age men. It's so taboo for these men to express their feelings and even pay attention to their health. Consequently, with the rise of prostate cancer in men, the situation calls for them take action. I think most men should consider the following questions:

- How often do you exercise?

- Are you comfortable doing what is necessary to take care of yourself?

Being a "man of a certain age" is not an excuse to give up on your physical appearance and health. Take the President of the United States, Barrack Obama. He is a prime example of a healthy and fit middle-aged man. He plays golf, basketball and he lives a healthy lifestyle. On the other hand, it's very taboo in certain cultures for men to get a manicure and pedicure. Imagine the stigma attached to getting a prostate exam. I think these men are suffocating in the debris of a cultural society that doesn't

edify them. Therefore, men shy away
from things that they feel may cause
others to question their sexuality. I em-
pathise with your situation. Each chapter will offer effective and practical
steps on how to love yourself more and
find true happiness. It doesn't matter
who you are, or what you do, start loving yourself and become a happier and
healthier you.

CHAPTER 3: LOVE YOURSELF FROM THE INSIDE OUT

Love and acceptance are the greatest gift you can give yourself. Whether you are male or female, it's important to love and accept yourself. Be reminded that you were fearfully and wonderfully made. You are perfect and your body is the greatest masterpiece you can have. Treat your body with respect. Avoid thoughts of rejection, guilt and depression. You are a gift to this world and you were created by God to reflect His glory and joy. Be mindful of what you speak about yourself. Your thoughts and words can easily manifest themselves. What you believe something to be, will become manifest if you do not change your thoughts. In other words, if all you speak is defeat and failure, you will never have the victory. Speak what you seek. Breathe life into your hopes and dreams and watch them take shape.

Once you have love and acceptance of self, there is no limit to what you can do. Loving yourself first makes it possible for others to do the same. Love and respect for self should become necessary. You may have been told you are a failure and you will never amount to anything, but I say life is a journey and it is never too late for a comeback. I have said many times that there is no such thing as failure, only "setbacks." Let every mistake be a lesson. The truth is setbacks are okay. They are just the universe's way of saying; try something better. Trust your heart and ignore the voice of doubt that can become so dominant in your thoughts.

You may be searching for something and you do not know what it is you are looking for. I encourage you to have the patience and in time it will be revealed to you. Put your faith in something greater than yourself. If you are not sure about your purpose, that is okay. Stop searching, pray about it and have the faith that it will be revealed to you. Give yourself a break and stop beating yourself up. Do not you think enough is enough? It's wrong to measure your achievements next to someone else. Each person walks a unique journey. Find your inner strength to rise above it all. Surround yourself with things that inspire you.

One key symptom of lack of self-love is when you feel absolutely alone. There is no reason to fear your own company. Your career can be on the right path and everything seem fine. Yet, something is missing. Are you still haunted by the past or do you fear the future? My advice is to let it go. You do not live in the past. Your place is here, in this very moment. You are doing yourself an injustice when you continue to beat yourself up. The only thing permitted to be dominate your mind is your goals and the steps you plan to take to achieve them. Release yourself of every hurt. Forgive yourself and forgive others. Forgiveness is not spontaneous. Instead, forgiveness is a process. It means, every time a hurtful memory resurfaces in your mind, you replace the hatred with thoughts of blessings and love. The result is that you will feel powerful and in control of your life. Love and forgiveness are the only weapons you need when you face certain difficulties.

Talk to someone who will be truly objective and has your best interests at heart. Sometimes you need someone to call you out on your faults. Confront the truth about yourself. The truth is you may be spending too much time "whining" about the same issue. When will you stop? Sometimes you must be willing to accept the fact that the reason you are angry with someone is because they have touched on a sensitive issue your reaction to it should be evaluated carefully. When you are pursuing your goals, never stop to respond to your critics. Were you calm and self-assured or were you angry and bitter. Always have something positive to say. Your critics are very smart so do not be gullible. Their only job is to distract you and make you upset. Always remind yourself their game is not intriguing enough. Set various goals for yourself and try to accomplish a new one each month. Distractions may surface, but the dream should never stop for anyone. Finally, I refer to a wonderful quote by Carl Jung: "Everything that irritates us about others can lead us to an understanding of ourselves." I always look within myself to decide what is causing me to feel irritated. Never allow pride block you from being well within.

Tips:

- Avoid feeling regret for purchases you make for your self –improvement. They are necessary for growth.

- Take time to reflect. Look back at yourself six months ago. Think about it for a minute. Look at yourself now. Think about it for a minute. What has changed? If something has changed write it down. If it's good, embrace it and build on it. If it's less than desirable, admit it, confront it and heal yourself by accepting you have allowed yourself to be hurt and knowing you can do better.

- "There is nothing better than coming back to where nothing has changed to understand how you've changed."-(Unknown)

CHAPTER 4: TRUE BEAUTY LIES WITHIN

The most beautiful women are those who have a beautiful heart even if they have been blessed with physical beauty. Having a pretty face means nothing if everything that comes out of your mouth is marked by sarcasm, hate, jealousy, bitterness and anger. True beauty is acceptance of self. Allow people to feel comfortable around you always. Showing kindness, love and appreciation for others is beauty in itself. Be kind to people. It's extremely rewarding when you show consideration for people's feelings. If you want respect from someone, you cannot demand it. Confront the truth about yourself first to determine why that person feels the way he or she does. You may feel within yourself that you have power and can intimidate others. However, be careful with power. To whom much is given much is taken away. You can foster peace and love with others when you show humility, love and kindness to others. It's best never to dismiss people. You could learn something from them.

A beautiful woman is clothed in strength and dignity. She is fearless. Her presence is magnetic and her very aura is revered. She lives and walks in light and love. To be a beautiful woman you must be comfortable in your own skin and completely accept who you are. The length of your hair, race, height or status does not define your identity and beauty. I look back on my time throughout high school and I was very uncomfortable with my height. Almost every girl in my class was of average height. The dichotomy in my life was my view of myself and society's view of how women are expected to be, which is further compounded by the good values my family instilled in me. Throughout my teens, I shied away from heels because "I am too tall." Presently, I love my heels and my body type is perfect. It does not matter if you are full figured or a size zero. True beauty reflects through the happy healthy glow you radiate and the joy of your smile. Deborah Barnes said: "True beauty radiates not from outer cosmetics, but from the simple joy of making a difference for those who need your voice, passion, and time without expecting or wanting anything in return."

What does God say about beauty?

God said we are all made in His image and we are all His children. There are many references of women in the Bible as being "beautiful." God also believes to be beautiful is to have the dignity, inner strength, grace and to be fearless (Proverbs 31:25). However, God does want His daughters to "adorn" themselves in modesty and appropriate clothing (1 Timothy 2:9). However, there is an error that many women make, whether Christians or believers, that God wants you to be "hideous". I once heard a woman say, "I am not the best looking woman, but I know how to present myself." It's not my place to determine who is beautiful. Others and myself agreed she carries herself with dignity, modesty and is an example to many women. Regardless if you are a Christian, you owe it to yourself to wear what is appropriate yet practical. Beautiful women are: moms, wives, daughters, sisters, aunts, cousins, friends, professionals, athletes, Christians, graceful, kind, loving, respectful, honest, trustworthy, happy, courageous, bold and more. Essentially beauty is relative and every woman should see herself as being beautiful. Even if you have been rejected in the past, remind yourself that God breathed life into you and He gave you an unique purpose. Therefore do not be defined by what people say you are, see yourself as how God sees you: created in his image to reflect his light and his glory.

There is a reason behind God creating you the way He did. Ultimately, as a Christian, your goal is to be a shining example so that non-believers can see the glory and joy of God reflecting through you. Another point to note is that beauty is being graceful even under the worst of circumstances. The most beautiful thing is to be able to bless others even when you are going through your biggest storms. It's a powerful feeling when you can love yourself from within and God's love wrap itself around you. Feeling and being fabulous is to feel strong, empowered, exclusive and feel youthful. I have explored the topic of "fabulosity" even deeper in my book *Fabulosity Is You: A Woman's Guide For Building Her Confidence, Fashion Tips, Weight Loss Tips, Skin Care Secrets, Relationships And Pursuing Her Purpose.*

What does society say about beauty?

Society says beauty is power. It also says that if you feel you lack the "elements" of beauty, it can be bought at a price. The media idolises celebrities of a certain physical makeup: women of average height with a size four or below. While many have worked extremely hard to change this perception, some beautiful young women who consider themselves overweight become bulimic and anorexic. Each time these cases, I wonder: who or what took away that young woman's self-respect? Sometimes the problem is purely psychological. The battle lies in the fact that you want to control your emotions and life. Instead of loving yourself, you may think self-esteem is based on how much you weigh and how thin you are. Happiness cannot be based on how thin a person looks. Consequently, you neglect your health. The psychological damage flashy commercials pushing women's beauty products and services cause can be repaired. However, there must be a willingness on your part to take new steps of change. Strive to be fit and healthy, not skinny.

A booming beauty and cosmetics industry tells me that too much emphasis is placed on physical beauty. You have to admit that the media plays a huge role in the shaping of lifestyles. As such, this culture of consumerism has left some of your daughters, sisters, mothers, and wives uncertain of whom they are. It communicates to some women that they should never accept their authentic self. The concept, "if it sags, snip it, fill it and repeat" has become the norm in some cultures. The result leaves much to be desired for some females, while for others it's just what they genuinely wanted to do. It can be for medical reasons, or a sincere desire to feel whole and complete. On the other hand, some young women will deplete their savings for plastic surgery.

Sadly, for some, the urge to alter their physical appearance has resulted in serious health problems. Essentially, if girls are taught good values, especially the importance of loving herself, it could mean the difference between a life of strength and purpose, or a life of self-destruction and death.

Tips:

- Stand before your mirror and really look at yourself. Accept the fact that you were wonderfully and fearfully made.

- Treat yourself to a day at the spa or bring the spa to your home by using one of my amazing homemade skin care secrets in the book *Fabulosity Is You: A Woman's Guide For Building Confidence, Fashion Tips, Weight Loss Tips, Skin Care Secrets, Re-*

lationships And Pursuing Her Purpose.

- Forgive the past and anyone who made you feel less than yourself and know that true beauty lies in your character.

CHAPTER 5: KNOW YOUR WORTH

Knowing your worth is crucial to your happiness. No one is permitted to treat you less than you are. However, they are not looking for your permission. Your greatest test is to remain steadfast in the belief that you are worthy of love and respect. You are a beautiful and unique masterpiece. You were designed to be equal, to be loved and protected by your partner in your life. If a person makes you constantly compare yourself to others, it's time to either confront the situation or walk away. Feel free to evaluate the people in your life and close some doors. Paul Coelho said: "Close some doors today. Not because of pride, incapacity, or arrogance, but simply because they lead you nowhere." Lead by example and show people that you deserve love and respect. Simply commanding someone to respect you is as useless as worrying. Be a woman of class. Be a man of dignity. Your style reflects class and your actions support this. Think, walk and act with integrity.

If someone refuses to commit to a relationship, let him or her go immediately. If it's meant to be, it will happen. When they do, set the chapters or boundaries. You may not realise this, but people can test you to see how much they can get away with. This means your worth is determined on what you accept. Take control of your life because it was given to you only. You cannot allow someone else to live it for you. Remind yourself that you are valuable and precious, and you are not to be treated as second rate. No one else can be like you. Live your life on your own terms. Anything you wanted to do and were afraid of, do it. Life is a series of memories, lessons and experiences, but the one thing you seek is happiness. To be happy is to know your worth. In everything you do, value yourself. You cannot live the results of other people. You determine what happens to you by what you believe about yourself.

One of the world's greatest inventors, Steve Jobs, said, "Your time is limited, so don't waste it living someone else's life. Don't be trapped by dogma – which is living with the results of other people's thinking. Don't let the noise of other's opinions drown out your own inner voice. Most important, have the courage to follow your heart and intuition. They somehow already know what you truly want to become. Everything else is secondary." Whatever happens, never surrender your power. Actor, Michael J. Fox said: "One's dignity may be assaulted, vandalised, and cruelly mocked, but it can never be taken away unless it is surrendered." Both men are brilliant in their fields. They battled life and death, but no matter what happened they never lost hope. Steve Jobs did fulfil his purpose and many say, a life well lived. Therefore, whether you have been bullied, abused, had your dignity attacked, or suffering from lack

of self-esteem, begin to feel empowered.

Please note that there are adults who
will try to bully you, male or female.
The need to bully others stems from
the need to overcome insecurities and
to feel in control. They try to strike
where you are the weakest and they
want you to play their game. Adult bul-
lies can be someone who likes to cause
disruption whether directly or indirect-
ly to see how you will respond. However, never underestimate the power of
silence—even if everything about your
being is telling you to respond. Remind
yourself that you will not be playing
that game and you will be reborn
stronger. No one is allowed to rain on
your joy and dreams. Forgive and release them. It's always best to respect
people, even if your ideals differ.

Tips:

- Remind yourself

you are loved and you are enough for you.

- If you love and value yourself, others will see your worth

CHAPTER 6: HAVE AN ATTITUDE OF GRATITUDE

Have an attitude of gratitude. Be grateful for what you have. Allowing your mind to be clouded by what you do not have will prevent you from experiencing gratitude. Giving thanks for the good in every bad situation allows you to surrender to gratitude. Having gratitude is to know that in the infinity of life, everything is okay. You are breathing, a new day is coming and you will have yet another chance to do things right. Whatever you do, do not hold yesterday against yourself. It's gone forever. Just think about now and the small steps you can take to live a life of gratitude. You need to release yourself of every chain of the past to experience fully abundance. Take a walk outside, look around you, feel the wind brush against your face, listen to the birds singing cheerfully, and absorb the beauty of nature. If you live in a city, visit a park where it's safe to be. There is peace and gratitude to be found in stillness. These are some of the little things not to ignore.

People with an attitude of gratitude to life have a natural glow about them. They emit love and light that can break through every barrier. Attitude is a critical skill that cannot be easily taught. Its how you "feel" about something. To put it simply, ask yourself: How do you feel about something in your life? If someone should ask me, how do you feel about life? I say, "I am thankful for it." There will be days when you feel uninspired which results in a bad attitude. It's also true that the negative energy from those around you could easily weigh you down. This could cause you to be pushed by your problems instead of being led by your dreams. Examine whether the person is important to you. If this is not the case, I suggest that you avoid such persons, as they bring no value to your life. Who you allow into your life needs to have a positive purpose.

Choose to have a positive attitude, which leads to a great day. Its one thing to say you are grateful, but do you practice having gratitude? Be thankful for everything, even if things are not going your way. Have faith in the situation and stay calm. Always handle stressful situations with grace and dignity and accept that it could change anytime. I am confident you have the capacity of doing so. A positive attitude is an art that must be continually re-shaped. This allows you to feel grateful about many things in your life.

Tips:

- When you awake in the morning, give thanks for the ability to breathe, to think and to be alive.

- Look at the beauty of the people in your life and the things you have been blessed with so far.

CHAPTER 7: BE BOLD, BE CONFIDENT

Confidence is a "certainty" you feel about something or someone. Everything about you radiate this joy and love and that makes others become drawn to you. Confidence is 90 percent your thoughts and ten percent your physical appearance. Negative thoughts and uncertainty makes you attract negative people and situations. You are attracting unfavourable events in your life because your face reflects that which you feel and you in turn look on others to trying to confirm if they are looking at you with judgment or ridicule. However, by healing your emotional and trust issues, you will begin to feel a joy and peace within. Give your mind a break because it needs to rest. Talk to someone you can trust and let go of everything that bothers you. You may not get a complete healing with one conversation, but you will feel much better. The next time you go out, make a deliberate effort to be kind to someone and keep a smile on your face. Do not be surprised if you see people smiling back. Leverage your present accomplishments to build your confidence. If you build on what you have, you are well on your way to become the successful individual I know you are meant to be.

When in doubt, simplicity is the ultimate form of sophistication. In *Fabulosity Is You: A Woman's Guide For Building Her Confidence, Fashion Tips, Weight Loss Tips, Skin Care Secrets, Relationships And Pursuing Her Purpose*, I mentioned, 'less is more.' The way you speak is also an important factor in demonstrating confidence. Like everything else, confidence must be practiced to master fully. Take small steps first and with time you will get better. There are several little things that you will have to consider before reaching that level of confidence. Being happy and comfortable with you is critical. Also, setting goals and having faith that they will succeed is critical.

Confidence in yourself means you have already succeeded before you even begin. Begin to see yourself as a success and remind yourself that you have the boldness. You may want to start a business, but you are afraid of what others will think. Work as if everyone is already in agreement with you. Take a leap of faith and be bold. It is important to take criticism and it takes great restraint not to respond in the way you are expected to react. Be humble and know that everyone you meet can teach you something new. Learn to turn every weakness into strength. If you are impatient, inconsistent, and boring, then you are not being passionate, flexible and responsible. Allowing people to place his or her unhappiness on you will prevent you from celebrating you. Take care of your mind, body and soul. Confidence is knowing your worth. Do not settle for less than you are worth! You deserve all the good in the world. Self-love is the greatest. You need to know that if you are looking for acceptance from people, you could be waiting a very long time. Be bold and set yourself apart from your critics. Self-confidence and achieving your goals are the greatest barriers to negativity. If you begin to conceive a goal, always remember what motivated you to do it in the first place. If you simply want to raise awareness and bring clarity to the hearts and minds of people, hold unto that thought and go about it. Just remember never give up on a dream just because of the time it will take to accomplish it. Have patience and enjoy the process. You will be very surprised how time goes by very quickly. Be confident and be beautiful.

Tips:

- Write down a small and achievable goal. Ensure that it is something you have always wanted to do. Think about what you need to do to put it into action. Avoid thinking about what others will think and do it.

• Have good intentions and keep them. Never abandon your goals. If you feel opposition you are close to your breakthrough.

CHAPTER 8: HAPPINESS IS FOUND IN THE MOMENTS

We all want to find happiness and ful-
filment. Is not happiness what everyone
dreams of? In trying to acquire wealth,
or find true love at the expense of your
own needs or those who care about
you, true happiness remains elusive.
You have a purpose in this life. If the
things you try result in "setbacks," try
something else, but enjoy the journey
along the way. As I discussed earlier,
those "setbacks" may turn out to be
"steps forward" on the path to your joy.
Remember to have the patience with
yourself. When you feel like you are in
the heat of battle with everything
crumbling around you, pause to remind
yourself it doesn't have to be a battle if
you continue to have hope and faith.

Setbacks do not mean you should
abandon your goals. Even when things
do not work out the way you wanted,

that does not mean they will not. Stressing or worrying about what is to come prevents you from living and enjoying your life today! When considering a major change because the place that you are in feels uncomfortable, look inside you and see what you can do to change your thoughts and attitude. As Dr. Wayne Dyer says, "What you focus on expands." Find more and more things to be grateful for. By focusing on what is missing from your life, you will find more and more things missing.

The past is the past. Looking back, and keeping your focus on the things that hurt you will only prevent you from living a happy life now. However, looking back to see the *lessons*, being grateful for the things each experience taught you, and forgiving yourself and those who hurt you, frees you up to enjoy every minute of every day that is given to you. Cherish the people in your life. Life is short, and one day you may look back on your life and say you wished you had loved more and enjoyed the little moments. Make use of your talents and take bold steps to doing what you love. Avoid regrets by fully living in each moment. Be happy with the woman you have become. Follow your convictions and be grateful for all you have. You just need to remember you are in a great place in your life. Tap into your inner most self through *stillness* or other activities and reconnect with yourself.

Tips:

- Think about something that is bothering you for one minute. Next, think about something positive and uplifting. No matter what emotion surfaces, begin to feel and observe it. If its good, your intuition will tell you.

- Focus on your strengths and think of ways to make them

better. Avoid criticising yourself if you have weaknesses. What positives can be found in them?

CHAPTER 9: DARE TO DREAM BIG AND NEVER QUIT!

I believe in setting goals. It is important to clarify and prioritise. You can have any number of goals, which can be short-term or long-term. Hold yourself accountable to your goals. Share them with the right people so they can cheer you on to success. If they do not, they are just part of a much bigger show. Your purpose is greater than you and setbacks are just part of the process to success. Remember to clarify and prioritise your goals. Clarifying your goal is having a structured process on how you plan to accomplish them. When you prioritise your goals you are ranking them in order of importance or most critical. You lose by setting goals. That is just the first step. Write them down or store them on your computer to serve as a reminder of what you want to achieve.

It does not hurt to consider how your goals will benefit you in the future. I would not suggest doing something solely for money unless it serves to the furthering of some other goal. Do what is necessary (legal and honest with integrity) to achieve your goals, while enjoying the process. Check your progress frequently to ensure you are on course. Have good intentions, commit and focus on one thing at a time. As you complete a task, adjust your goals. Speak about them in strong and certain terms. Speak about your goals with authority. Command the universe to send favours your way. If you encounter opposition, stand your ground and naysayers, doubt, fear and defeat will submit.

Separate what is important from what is not. Eliminate distractions, motivate yourself and be fuelled by the success of accomplishing each goal. Do not be surprised when you reach your goals faster than expected. This can also save valuable time. You may also find that you are motivated by each success. Besides saving time, you will reduce the stress on yourself and those around you. Allow your vision of who you want to be to take you places.

Tips

- Will you like yourself and what you are doing 20 years from now?

- Do I need additional skills and training in order to achieve my goals?

- Are any self-limiting thoughts holding me back?

- Will I enjoy myself in this next phase of my life?

CHAPTER 10: BE FABULOUS!

To be fabulous is to love yourself and know that you are amazing. You may not know it, but you are in an incredible place in your life right now. Whether you are faced with a decision or having a life changing experience, you now have what it takes to overcome it. Love and relationships are not supposed to be a battle. If you happen to be single, you do not have to subscribe to every "expert" who encourages women to be "players." This forces you to have a hardened perception of what love, relationships and marriage are all about. How do you expect a relationship to flourish if there is no friendship? I believe if you feel you are at war with yourself or someone else, just stop. Avoid playing games or being manipulated into one. You will find the right person at the right time. I recommend that you walk away from anything or anyone that is not contributing to your happiness. The choice is yours to make. No matter how devastating and hurtful the situation may be, never allow bitterness and anger to overcome you. Instead send love, light and blessings. By doing this, you have freed yourself and if that individual does not change, he or she will face his or her own Karma. I want to remind never allow yourself to be bitter. This could easily lead to depression. Break off the spirit of heaviness from over you. Stay connected with people and choose to see the beauty of life as it evolves around you. Therefore, treat yourself to something wonderful or a new significant experience. Watch your circle of friends and be mindful of the persons who are not looking out for your best interests.

To be fabulous you have to believe it. Toss away any feelings of rejection and push yourself towards accepting yourself and nurture a positive attitude. You were meant to do amazing things for yourself and others. However, I believe you must empower yourself fully first to stand against a changeable world. Fabulous people always have a positive energy to others and attract positive things and people. Willing something to happen will only make you frustrated. Remind yourself always to look and feel your best. Whether you are male or female, you owe it to yourself to put yourself first. Truly love and appreciate yourself and become a happier more empowered you.

Tips:

- You do not need a reason to look and feel fabulous. Go have a date with yourself for once. Have that drink you always wanted to try. Buy yourself some beautiful flowers.

- Take photos of

yourself when you feel
you are happiest. That way
if you ever feel less than
fabulous, you will have ev-
idence of your true au-
thentic self.

CHAPTER 11: LET CONFUSION BE A THING OF THE PAST!

"Someday everything will make perfect sense. So, for now, laugh at the confusion, smile through the tears and keep reminding yourself that everything happens for a reason"(Unknown). Sometimes you will be very confused, but never panic. You can either respond or react. Response suggests calmness and clarity, while reaction implies impulsiveness. You give power to any situation based on your reaction to it. Confusion will occur, but it will not remain. Learn to recognise it when it shows its ugly self. You may face a difficult decision of choosing between two jobs, someone may be deliberately trying to confuse you or you may simply be at a point contemplating a new direction. When you have measured your decision against every practical solution, the final deciding factor will always be intuition. Trusting your "gut feeling" can sometimes lead to great things. Avoid mistaking doubt for fear. The presence of fear means you are on the right track, but you need to have the faith in yourself. All these things contribute to confusion. All you can do is live in the now. Make use of every day. Each new day brings a blank sheet of paper for you to write something significant for your life. Use it wisely!

Even though you will go through all the pain, sadness and hurt, one day you will emerge happier, stronger, confident and victorious. If you are a Christian, stand on God's word and remind him of his promise. God restores, liberates, increases and will give you a life of abundance. How deep is your faith? You may be living in a moment where everything is hopeless. Speak to God and ask him for guidance. His love is endless, powerful and much bigger than the problems that you face. I always say that God happens when you put faith before fear. Faith in God is everything. You will win. God wants you to be at peace with the past and so you can be comforted.

Whatever is meant to be will be, but only you can determine if you want to be happy in the future. Once you make a firm decision to let confusion be a thing of the past, you will unlock the door to gratitude. Surrender everything to God and know that you do things, not by your will, but by his will. With gratitude, you will begin to experience life. Gratitude is acceptance, clarity and abundance. Having a sense of gratitude counteracts confusion. Nothing can breathe, exist or thrive where there is chaos and confusion. t stifles growth and happiness. If you find that you are repeating the past, its time to change your future. Nothing is wrong with self-preservation at times. Always remember that self-preservation is an asset since you do not completely alienate those who love you. Accept the fact that some people and situations will only remain as lessons learnt. Living contentment and gratitude is a choice you can make. Choose wisely. This is an affirmation I coined and has used many times:

"From this day forward, I will not allow confusion to be the order of my day. I will live in gratitude for all my life. My life radiates the joy, light, gratitude and peace." –Winsome Campbell-Green

Tips:

- Be still. Take 15 minutes out of your day to clear your mind of all the chatter. Find a quiet place and allow yours muscles to relax, while breathing in and out. As you breathe in through your nostrils, tell yourself you are allowing love, light, gratitude, peace and abundance into your life. Inhale slowly. As you breathe out through your mouth, tell yourself you are letting go of confusion, chaos, doubt and fear. Exhale slowly.

- Change your approach. Chaos cannot meet chaos. If the problem bothers you, look on the situation and yourself objectively. Think about how you are reacting. Are you feeling angry, betrayed or misunderstood? Immediately forgive the person or situation and allow inner peace to flow through you

- Be authentic

- If you are not confident at public speaking, take lessons.

- Dress for the job you want

- Be mindful of your

thoughts. Your thoughts create your reality. Always think good things about yourself and others

- Be good to yourself and others

- A positive attitude is the ultimate weapon against any life challenge

- Pursue your purpose one goal at a time

- God will perfect all the things that concern you. Have patience

- You were born to win.

AUTHOR BIO

I am a multi-talented young woman who has a passion for writing and inspiring people. I hold a Bachelor of Arts Degree in with very high honours and hope to change thoughts and lives of people with my books. Currently I am working on more books that will provide my readers with even greater insight into the challenges that they are facing. I hope to inspire young adults (male and female), especially women, who have struggled to find their true purpose in life and who now want to live a life of strength, promise, purpose, power and potential. I am happily married to my best friend, who is my loving husband, and enjoy traveling and experiencing different cultures. Being the cheerful woman that I am, I believe in celebrating life and accept each day

with gratitude, love and a positive attitude. My hope is that my books will
continue to inspire and uplift readers
from all over the world.

NOTE FROM THE AUTHOR

It's with gratitude that I would like to thank you for reading *The 11 Chapters Of Self-Love for Women and Men: How To Be Present In Your Life and Achieve Happiness*. I truly hope that this book has been helpful. If you have enjoyed reading this book, please consider leaving a review on Amazon. It would be helpful to other readers and to me. Other books written by me include:

- *Ten Life Changing Lessons*

- *The Perks Of A Positive Attitude: A Practical Guide To Happiness And Success*

- *Fabulosity Is You! A Woman's Guide For Building Her Confidence, Fashion Tips, Weight Loss Tips, Skin Care Secrets, Relationships*

And Pursuing Her Purpose.

- *High Heels In Tech: Women, Technology And Change*

All available at: www.cgwritingservices.-com